# A QUIET WORLD

*Whispers of the Heart through*
*Poetry and Photography*

Sheri Quintana

Printed in the United States of America
Published in Hellertown, PA

Cover and interior design by Anna Magruder

Library of Congress Control Number 2022916806
ISBN 978-1-958711-18-7
2 4 6 8 10 9 7 5 3 1

For more information or to place bulk orders, contact the author or Jennifer@BrightCommunications.net.

To my dad, known to most as Poppy.
I love and miss you so much.

## Chiseled Journey

Animated and vibrant,
Unceasingly carving the earth with assured direction.

Sloped terrain forces momentum to build and buoys
determination forward.

What interferes with its course is merely a detour to recognize
a necessary truth,
Or to forge a new adventure.

Each dissolve into swells of wisdom,
integral to the journey ahead.

## Nature's Journal

Wisdom and secrets transcending time,
Witness to untold yesterdays.

An essence chiseled by harsh and harmonious cycles.
Telling tales of legendary journeys
And voyages into worldly wonders.

A shadow becomes shelter,
Silently holding space
For you to witness the majesty of your soul.

## Never Without

I emerge from the hush of a sleepy morn to share my dreams.
And without speaking,
You understand my aspirations.

I bow to the force of a rambunctious wind.
And without breaking,
I square my shoulders to a new confidence.

I echo the infectious melody of Mother Nature's bounty.
And without pause,
You match the rhythmic cadence of its familiarity.

I transcend the boundaries of rigid humility.
And without hesitation,
I saturate the soil with untethered mastery.

I call to the potential of your muted spirit.
And without sound,
You can hear Heaven's whispers.

# And Shadows Disappear

You wake,
Resuscitating the night from its still hibernation.

Sunrise gives witness to phenomenal possibilities,
Sharing a kiss of promise, hope, and inspiration.

And shadows disappear.

Surrendering to inner wisdom and guidance,
The masterpiece of Presence emerges.

Sunset gives pause to anchor this sacred evolution
With an exclamation of both colorful celebration
and peaceful grace.

And shadows disappear.

## This Moment

An ethereal refrain urges us to honor our days
            With importance and awareness.
 For it is this moment that matters most—
            And holds unequaled power
To dream and to create our tomorrows.

# When the World is Quiet

As loud as expectations
        and obligations
                and commitments
                        and responsibilities can be,
        there is a hushed resonance, impatiently waiting to be
        reawakened and heard.


Its language is compassion
                and kindness
                        and grace
                                and love.
        When the world is quiet,
        you recognize the yearning in your heart.

## I Dream

I dream of the forest.

Woody perfume saturates the air
And fills my core with newness and promise.

Sprawling shade trees and delicate vegetation
Insulate my intrusive thoughts and nourish my curious soul.

I detach from this frenzied world
And breathe in the silence of now.

## The Power of Silence

My voice is often misunderstood.
Words do not come easily
     and rarely describe my unique existence accurately.

Silence becomes my retreat.

I can be with what I know and what I feel—
without the need to explain or share or defend,
     without the need for any definition.

## Welcome Change

Where there is rigidity, there is stagnation,
and growth cannot be sustained
Welcome change—
a constant variable and often necessary force
to propel us forward.

## We Become

We embody the physical
And embark on an adventure
Of remembering and accepting
Our innate abilities
And integration with all that is.

## Is It Fate?

Experiences are not all fated.
However, each brings insight and direction
To uncover your full potential.

## The Summit

As I near the summit,
        a healing presence embraces me.

I harvest stars and moonlight from the night sky
        and instinctively absorb their secrets.

My soul attunes to their omniscience,
        and paradigms collapse.

# My Own Rules

I heard this in my head one day, sitting with my thoughts:
"You're not a rule breaker," it said, "so make your own, you ought."

Can I do that?
"Of course you can," a friend assured me with a text.

"What are you waiting for?" she questioned me,
"So, tell me then, what's next?"

It's not like I set out to cause some friction with the law.
But rather started questioning everything I saw.

And what I knew and how I thought: The truth was in my heart.
I'll put me first, do things my way, and this was just the start.

I found my strength, my inner voice, the whole of being Me.

My life is what I make of it.
My rules, my destiny.

# Firefly

Against a silhouette of trees,
tiny bursts of light pierce the dark blue sky

Carrying stardust on their wings,
Shimmering,
Whimsically,
Dancing,
They sprinkle the air with infectious merriment
and impish abandon.

## The Infectious Laugh

Quiet giggles innocently find traction
        and swell into muffled snickers.

Contagious.
        All effort to douse its energy is futile.

Helpless smirks infect others.
        Snickers become chuckles.
        Chuckles become side splitting, belly laughs.

Uncontrollable.

It morphs into life of its own,
        holding everyone at the mercy
        of the imminent snort.

Raucous laughter escalates into a breath-taking,
        mouth gaping, body convulsing,
        tears-rolling-down-the-face catharsis.

Gradually, the hysterics evaporate into
        casual banter and silly grins.

Exhausted and exhilarated,
        the uproar is a welcomed escape.

## Rocky Mountains

Standing upon layers of time,
      I'm left breathless by an unrestrained process of what
      is meant to be.

A sense of fearless presence.

A connectedness that makes a strong whole.

Never resistance.

Always accepting what is and adapting to accommodate
      change and growth.

Conflict recedes when trust and faith are reciprocal.

# Keepsakes

Driving on a winding, country lane without a destination,
  stopping to pick wildflowers and
  drinking from a roadside natural spring.

Sitting by a winding creek with a stick-and-string fishing pole,
  talking about family I never met but knew in my heart
  and laughing at nonsensical things until my cheeks hurt.

Stopping at the "money bridge" that Pa discovered
  when I was a child and collecting the coins that
  magically appeared there.

Waiting for Granny to call to tell me the cabbage and noodles
  is done and to bring my biggest pot to fill.

Calling Dad to ask him, yet again, how to relight the furnace
  and to diagnose what's wrong with my car—just by the
  noise it was making.

Cherished keepsakes.
  Legacies and memories.
    Chapters in my story.

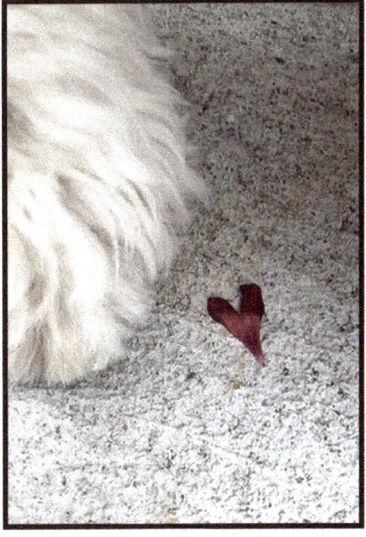

## The White Nightgown

I sensed Nanny close to me.
Her energy unmistakable, strong, wise, and maternal.

Generally fleeting in my awareness,
Today she lingered deliberately. Why did this feel different?

On the third day, she sent me a vision.
I saw her rocking a small boy in a white gown.

Later that afternoon, my dad unexpectedly passed away.

As memories were shared and recounted,
What I experienced became clear.

Dad was Nanny's favorite.
He was the only one as a small child allowed to wear her white nightgown when he slept over.

She had been waiting to hold and comfort him again.
This time, she would welcome him Home.

# Acknowledgments

I want to whole-heartedly thank Jennifer Bright and her entire team at Bright Communication for holding my hand, guiding and assisting me, and publishing my book. The synchronicity in our meeting was an obvious sign for me to finally bring it into fruition. Our visions were so wonderfully aligned! Big hugs to all of you!

I created this book as a leap of faith in myself; a way to fully express who I am. I consciously acknowledge that I have played life cautiously for a very long time and while that has served me well enough—I am blessed in many ways—I know there is so much more to experience as I embrace all of me.

I am happiest when I am in a creative space, whether that be doing arts and crafts, taking photos of things I love, enjoying deep, intellectual stimulation, or bringing to life my inspired visions.

I share with you *A Quiet World* in hopes that you will honor who you are. Is it time to do something different? Is there something you've always wanted to do? Are you doing the things you enjoy? Do you want to have more fun?

Listen to your heart and celebrate all of you!

Live fully, love fully, and be all of what and who you are!
The world needs you!

# About the Author

Sheri Quintana is a Reiki Master/Teacher, wife, mother of two grown children, and a dog mom. She adores all animals, wildlife, nature, mountain streams, and the beauty and energy they all share. Sheri is proud of the innovative and resourcefulness of her creative pursuits, which can be seen in her home, garden, and crafts. And, if power tools are involved, even better! She is also a self-taught drummer.

Sheri's first visit to the Colorado Rocky Mountains inspired this book. Natural elements "spoke" to her, initially resulting in very imaginative, vibrant, passages infused with life-force (Reiki) energy. The poems organically shifted to very personal and emotional experiences.

www.ingramcontent.com/pod-product-compliance
Lightning Source LLC
Chambersburg PA
CBHW041525120626
46551CB00018B/2574